Nathaniel's Journey

Written By:
Michelle Spalding

Illustrated By:
Shay Page

Sarah —

Sometimes showing up differently helps us see things more clearly ♡

love

MS

ISBN: 978-1-7347146-1-6

Copyright © 2022 Michelle Spalding

All rights reserved. No part of this book may be reproduced, stored, or transmitted by any means—whether auditory, graphic mechanical, or electronic—without written permission of the author, except in the case of brief excerpts used in critical articles and reviews. Unauthorized reproduction of any part of this work is illegal and is punishable by law.

This story is fiction. All of the characters, names, incidents, organizations, and dialogue in this novel are either the products of the author's imagination or are used fictitiously.

Happy Zinnia
Publishing

To all who wonder if you're on the right path
- you are, I promise.

Nathaniel felt a sort of calling nudging him to venture back to earth. While he was happy where he was, and things were good, he knew it was time. Nathaniel was what many would call an 'old soul,' having been to earth many times; there he'd learned many lessons, loved many people, and experienced many unforgettable things. Because of all those experiences, he knew exactly the life he wanted to live this time.

Joy and excitement unlike any he'd felt before filled Nathaniel–it was even bigger than that time he had gotten a new puppy.

He knew this time would be the best yet, and he raced to tell the Great Omnipotent Divine, usually known as God.

Nathaniel said, "I'm ready now, and I know exactly what I'd like to experience. First, it is important to me to learn to stand tall, be proud of who I am, and be a productive member of my society. I'd like to experience all four seasons and spend lots of time in nature. It would be nice to spend time around those who are like-minded but also to experience the contrast of others who see the world differently. And I feel it's essential to me to experience love in a multitude of different ways. Oh, and I think I'd like to stay for a while this time, maybe a hundred years give or take."

God said, "Excellent, Nathaniel, those experiences sound marvelous. I'll get everything started for your next adventure right now. I'm proud of you and the lessons you've chosen. I am looking forward to being a part of the adventure with you."

Nathaniel enthusiastically thanked God, and the next thing he knew, he was in a dark, warm place. He could hear sounds around him but couldn't really understand what was being said.

Even in the dark and not knowing what he was in for, he was at ease and happy to be back on earth for this new adventure.

Time is a funny thing on earth. To humans, it's generally about getting somewhere and doing something at a specific time on the calendar and clock.

It's a useful measuring tool to keep the peace, and it's helpful in making sure that people feel in control. Nathaniel spent several months in this dark warm place before one day bursting forth and seeing the sunlight as it washed over him.

The warmth of the sun felt good, and as he strained to look around at the form he'd been given, Nathaniel was quite shocked and disappointed to discover that he was a baby tree. Was this a cruel joke? Could God have made a mistake? Nathaniel thought he'd made it pretty clear what he wanted to experience.

"This is never going to work!" he cried aloud, but in his small form tucked away in the forest, no one heard him.

What could Nathaniel accomplish as a tree? He was not happy and thought about asking God for a 'do-over.' Then he could come back as something more practical for the adventures he'd wanted to experience. Poor me, Nathaniel thought, there is no way I'll be able to do any of the things that I requested while I'm here as just a tree. There's no one to love, no community or connection. Yes, he had told God he wanted to spend lots of time in nature, but this was ridiculous. If he'd come as a child to kind parents, he'd experience familial love. If he'd belonged to a family of immigrants, he'd experience compassion and learn to stand tall. Or if he'd been born to a family that lived on a hippy commune, he'd learn to be a productive part of a close-knit community and to care for others.

How on earth can I ever experience anything significant as just a tree? he pondered

The life of a tree is rather fixed. Where the seed lands in the earth is generally where the plant must stay until its time is up. There is no moving to a new location when the plant gets tired of this one or the neighbors nearby. It can't go south when the weather is frigid or closer to water when there is a drought. Very few can hear a tree or truly communicate with it, so even when it speaks up, it's like talking into the wind. Nope, a tree is where it is for the long haul, so somehow, one must make the best of it. And that's what Nathaniel tried to do: he did his best to focus on growing, knowing lots of little sprouts never made it to full trees.

All around Nathaniel were majestic trees that were often admired by the visitors who strolled through the forest. Initially, he was peeved that people didn't notice him. "Hello, can't you see me here struggling to grow?" he would often say aloud. Then as the years went by, he developed some patience with himself and others. This wasn't easy, as so many things were beyond his control as a tree, such as who he spent time with, what he could see, or even who would listen or comfort him when he cried.

Year after year, Nathaniel grew larger and taller until one day he too was a majestic tree with a trunk so big that no human could wrap its arms around him.
Most people don't realize it, but trees talk, usually to one another through an underground network of roots. Nathaniel loved to hear the stories that the elder trees told of the things they'd witnessed in the past.

The elders told stories of the many people who had visited them and even of some special ones whom they could communicate with. They told stories of harsh winters they'd endured and how some of their branches didn't make it when the temperatures were below freezing for extended periods. They spoke of the time when a drought coupled with a carelessly dropped cigarette had threatened to wipe out the whole forest. Stories of the fires always scared Nathaniel until the elder trees got to the part about the brave firefighters who came to battle the flames and saved much of the forest as well as the many different creatures that shared the woods.

Nathaniel lived in a very popular area that brought many visitors throughout the seasons. Some were regulars and visited often; others only came once. He greeted each one as they approached him. A few stopped and touched his trunk, letting him know they'd heard him.

In the summer, people picnicked under his large canopy of leaves where they were shaded from the bright sun. Summers were relaxing times in the forest when visitors often sat near him reading books, taking naps, or chatting with friends. He especially enjoyed watching the kids play games.

In the fall, visitors flocked to the forest to admire the colorful display of his leaves as they changed from green to gold to red before falling off completely. Nathaniel was always amazed at how buzzing the forest was with humans and these strange devices they carried to capture what they called pictures. Sometimes they seemed to spend more time doing that than really being present during the very short time they had to see the fall foliage. After all, it took a lot of energy for the trees to coordinate this spectacle, and they couldn't keep it up for long.

In the winter, there were often people nearby making snow angels or having snowball fights. Occasionally, when the winters were exceptionally cold, there were days, even weeks when Nathaniel would see no one. This made him feel sad and reminded him of how stuck a tree is. He especially missed the regulars, and he would worry about them if he hadn't seen them for a while, wishing he could somehow check on them. Thankfully, they always came back when the weather was more favorable.

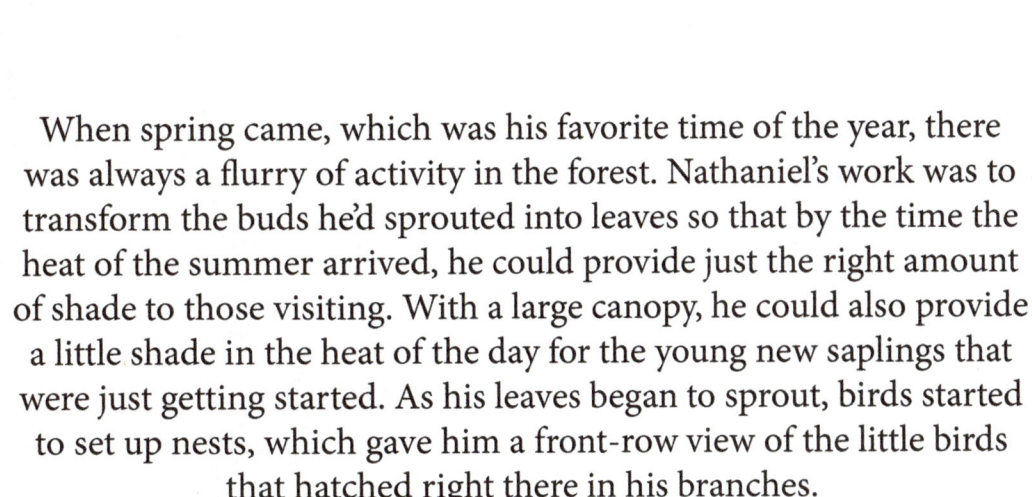

When spring came, which was his favorite time of the year, there was always a flurry of activity in the forest. Nathaniel's work was to transform the buds he'd sprouted into leaves so that by the time the heat of the summer arrived, he could provide just the right amount of shade to those visiting. With a large canopy, he could also provide a little shade in the heat of the day for the young new saplings that were just getting started. As his leaves began to sprout, birds started to set up nests, which gave him a front-row view of the little birds that hatched right there in his branches.

Year after year, season after season, he did much the same thing. And while it was a good life for a tree, he always struggled with the request he had made before coming back to earth and how different his life was from what he'd anticipated. Nathaniel often played and replayed the conversation in his head, wondering how his request could have gotten so mixed up.

One day when he'd been a tree for a long while, he finally said to God, "I'm struggling and feel like I wasn't heard. I don't see how I'll ever learn any of the lessons I desired or have the experiences I'd hoped for, beyond being in nature; can you please help me out?"

God replied, "Yes, of course, I'm glad you finally asked."
God explained: as Nathaniel had grown, he'd become proud of who he was and stood tall. He'd spent his days with others who were like-minded, and there were always many creatures nearby to provide contrast; didn't he remember the times when forest animals had used him as a scratching post or urinal? That was certainly some contrast! And few but a tree had more intimate experiences seeing the four seasons. Nathaniel got to live and breathe them day in and day out along with others in the forest, which is exactly a community.

"Okay," Nathaniel said to God, "But what about love? I don't see how anyone could love a silly tree or experience the love I wished to share."

"Ah, Nathaniel, you sweet soul, let me show you," said God. "First and foremost, you are loved by me," God explained, "and as the Divine Creator, I have sent others here who are like you and are able to show you love."

"Do you remember when you were a small tree and you were trying hard to grow, and the older trees helped to shade you when the sun was too hot in the summer? How they told you stories, and when you were scared, they comforted you? That, my friend, is Love. The firefighters who came to the area and battled the forest fire to save you and others in the forest? That, my friend, is Love. Oh, remember when the children danced and sang around you? And that time the adorable curly-haired little girl shared her juice with you? Much to her mother's chagrin, she said you had told her you were thirsty, so she poured the entire family's picnic worth of juice in a circle around your roots. That, my friend, is Love. How about the birds who built nests in your branches year after year so they could be close to you? That, my friend, is Love."

I know that you remember the couple who used to visit the forest and sit under your branches and talk for hours. I've heard you talk about them many times, how he proposed there while they were resting against your trunk. Year after year they would come back to visit you, later bringing along their own children. That, my friend, is Love. I could go on and on, but as you can see, you've experienced many different expressions of Love in your lifetime, most of which you would not know if you'd come here for this adventure in human form."

Nathaniel said to God, "It was there all along, and I almost missed it, thinking I'd come into the wrong form, thinking there was a mistake."

God replied, "I know, and it's okay. That's why they are called lessons."

The next few years were truly some of Nathaniel's favorites. While they were not much different from the years past, he was seeing them in a new light. For the first time, he was delighted to be there in his life as a tree. He became an elder and was bestowed the honor of sharing stories with the younger trees–his stories were always forest favorites.

A while later, Nathaniel realized that his time on earth as a big beautiful tree was coming to an end. He began saying goodbye to his friends in the forest and enjoyed one last joy-filled spring.

Later that summer, a fire raged through the woods, and although firefighters tried hard to save the forest, Nathaniel knew it was time to go. In almost an instant, the form in which he had learned so much was no longer, and immediately he returned to spirit form.

Upon his return, he was met by God, as all souls are after their time on earth.

God welcomed him and told him,
"Let me know when you're ready for your next adventure."

The End

Several years ago, while hiking in the foothills of the Georgia mountains, this story came to me. It had been a few years since I'd experienced the spectacle of fall, and when I picked up a leaf to admire the magnificent colors it displayed, I felt the urge to write. Shortly after returning to our cabin for the day, I captured this story on my computer.

Michelle Spalding is an author, coach, and business alchemist. When she's not working with clients or writing you can often find her curled up with a cup of tea reading a book or playing with the Grand Ginger. She currently lives in Waco, TX.

Connect with her online at www.MichelleSpalding.com

CPSIA information can be obtained
at www.ICGtesting.com
Printed in the USA
BVHW021441210622
640257BV00002B/5